The Ten Suns and the Moon

by Trish Marx

illustrated by Cheryle Kirk Noll

HARCOURT
SCHOOL PUBLISHERS

D1797539

Printed in China

ISBN 10: 0-15-350323-8
ISBN 13: 978-0-15-350323-8

Ordering Options
ISBN 10: 0-15-349941-9 (Grade 6 ELL Collection)
ISBN 13: 978-0-15-349941-8 (Grade 6 ELL Collection)
ISBN 10: 0-15-357369-4 (package of 5)
ISBN 13: 978-0-15-357369-9 (package of 5)

5 6 7 8 9 10   0940   15 14 13 12 11 10 09

Many years ago, there was a land where ten suns shone in the sky all day long! This land was China. The suns were very hard on the land. Rivers dried up until they became beds of dust. Rice and wheat plants withered, turned brown, and fell to the ground. The people were starving.

"What can we do?" the villagers cried. They called a meeting and decided their only hope was to ask Shen-Shu for help. Shen-Shu was the best in the land with a bow and arrow. "Please, shoot the suns down from the sky, Shen-Shu," the villagers begged him.

3

Shen-Shu was a kind man. He agreed to help. He climbed to the top of the highest mountain in China. The villagers followed him and cheered as he took an arrow from the case on his back. They cheered again as he shot the arrow to the first sun. They cheered the loudest when the sun fell from the sky and disappeared forever.

Shen-Shu took a second arrow from the case. Again, a sun fell from the sky and vanished. Then he shot a third arrow, and a fourth, never missing his targets. He reached for his last arrow after he had shot the ninth sun down. The tenth arrow wasn't there! A wise old man had taken it. He knew the last sun was needed for warmth and life on earth. Shen-Shu searched for a long time, but he did not find the arrow. Finally, he walked down the mountain. Everyone cheered and called him a hero!

Someone else was also watching—Queen Mother of the West, the wife of the all-powerful Chinese god. She rewarded Shen-Shu's bravery and strength by naming him Emperor of China. Then she gave him a packet of seeds. "These are special seeds," she said. "They will make you live forever. However, eat only one seed at a time, or something will happen that can never be changed."

Shen-Shu ruled wisely and well for a long time. He would eat one of his special seeds every once in a while to keep himself young. He gave his people fine fields for their crops and sturdy horses and oxen to pull their plows. He built them snug homes with warm hearth fires. He promised market days for selling and trading, and festival days for song and dance. Everyone was happy. Eventually, Shen-Shu met a thoughtful and kind woman named Ming, and they married. They were very happy and content for a time, carefully ruling over the people of China.

   Shen-Shu eventually became bored because
everyone in China was so satisfied. He counted his
money to amuse himself. Before long, he could think
of nothing else but his stacks and stacks of gold coins.
He forgot about his subjects and what they needed. He
sent away anyone who tried to see him because of a
problem. If it rained too much and the rivers flooded, he
refused to provide food and warm clothing. If insects
ate the crops, he shut his palace doors and feasted on
the fine food he had stored for himself.

His wife, Ming, was a good woman with a kind heart. She had all the good qualities that her husband lacked. Ming was greatly saddened by the change in her husband's behavior. She pleaded for him to help his people. Shen-Shu listened to her pleas because he loved his wife very much. He would send carts filled with rice, fruits, and vegetables to the country villages for a few days. Then he would forget and go back into his room filled with gold.

"Think back to the kindness you once showed," Ming begged. Shen-Shu tried harder to remember. He put aside his stacks of gold and bought bright silk robes for Ming. She would not wear them. He gave her ropes of pearls and beautiful green jade necklaces and bracelets. However, she sold them for money for the poor. He ordered special teas and sweets. She refused to eat them.

"I do not want these gifts," she told Shen. "I want the one thing I cannot have—a wise and good husband who watches over his people. What has happened to that man? Now all you do is count your riches. Do you not remember how you once cared for your people? Do you not recall the great things you did for China?"

Ming was worried that she would never be able to change Shen-Shu back into the kind emperor who had shot the suns from the sky. "My husband will not change," she said to herself. "I must do something to stop him from being a greedy, uncaring leader to the people of China."

Then she had an idea. She needed to find the special seeds given to Shen-Shu by the Queen Mother of the West. Shen-Shu would no longer have the power to live forever without the seeds. He could not continue to be a bad ruler. Ming searched and searched until she found the seeds. She grabbed the packet and ran from the palace.

Shen-Shu panicked and called his guards when he saw his wife fleeing from the palace. "Bring her back," he shouted. "However, please be careful. I don't want her to be hurt."

Ming knew there was only one escape from the guards on their horses who swooped down to grab her. She opened the packet. Then she swallowed every single seed in one big gulp. Shen-Shu followed closely behind his guards. He saw Ming swalllow the seeds.

Only then did Shen-Shu remember the Queen's warning: "Take only one at a time, or something will happen that can never be changed."

"No!" he shouted. However, it was too late. Ming was already floating above the guards. Her silken robes rippled in the wind. Shen-Shu watched with sadness as his wife rose higher, as if she had hidden wings. She grew smaller and smaller until she landed on the moon. Shen-Shu finally realized his mistake. He vowed never again to forget his people. Today Ming still lives on the moon, smiling down on earth, on Shen-Shu, and on her beloved people of China.

Scaffolded Language Development

USING VERBS Remind students that there are no spelling rules for putting irregular verbs in the past tense. They simply have to memorize these forms. Teach or review the past tense of the following irregular verbs:

become → became   feel → felt   shoot → shot

bring → brought   hear → heard   stand → stood

drink → drank   lead → led   steal → stole

fall → fell   make → made   take → took

Have students practice these spelling forms by holding a spelling bee, or have pairs of students practice with each other by using flashcards with the present tense on one side of a card and the past tense on the other.

 Social Studies

Research China Have students research China and list five interesting facts about the country. Then have students share their facts and see how many different facts about China they have collected.

School-Home Connection

Lessons Taught Have students share this story with a friend or family member. Ask them to talk about what lesson the author was trying to teach in the story.

Word Count: 1,037